COLOR HIKING GUIDE

MOUNT RAINIER

ALAN KEARNEY

COLOR HIKING GUIDE TO
MOUNT RAINIER

Alan Kearney

Frank
Amato
PORTLAND

About the Author

CARL SKOOG PHOTO

Alan Kearney grew up in the Northwest and began hiking, skiing and climbing mountains at the age of seven. He has been publishing photographs and writing articles about the outdoors since 1975. His work has appeared in *Climbing, Rock and Ice, Men's Health, Newsweek* and *Outside*. His first book *Mountaineering In Patagonia* was published in 1993. He resides in Bellingham, Washington where he writes and shoots photos full time.

Acknowledgements

I would like to thank my mom (Marianna Kearney) for joining me on several of the hikes in this book and contributing her writings of Shriner's Peak and Naches Peak. Jodi Broughton edited the manuscript and provided objective advice in many parts. Russ Lee edited the text with a special eye on the photography comments I had written. Thanks also go to Mike Lee, Kathy Swindler, Sue Hindman and Roberta Lowe for helpful opinions.

I am grateful to my parents for introducing me to the outdoors and encouraging my writing and photography for the past 18 years.

©1999 Alan Kearney

All rights reserved. No part of this book may be reproduced in any means without the written consent of the Publisher, except in the case of brief excerpts in critical reviews and articles.

Published in 1999 by:
Frank Amato Publications, Inc.
PO Box 82112 • Portland, Oregon 97282 • (503) 653-8108

Softbound ISBN: 1-57188-180-8   Softbound UPC: 0-66066-00382-9

Photography by Alan Kearney unless otherwise noted.
Book Design: Amy Tomlinson
Cover photo: Hiker near Paradise Creek in autumn.
Page 1: Mount Rainier and the Mowich face at dusk from Tolmie Peak.
Pages 2-3: Backpacker in Indian Henry's Hunting Ground after an early October snowfall.

Printed in Hong Kong
1   3   5   7   9   10   8   6   4   2

CONTENTS

Silver Falls on the Ohanapecosh River.

Hiker en route to Panorama Point.

Huckleberry leaves glow in the evening light on Shriner Peak.

Comet Falls

MOUNT RAINIER NATIONAL PARK

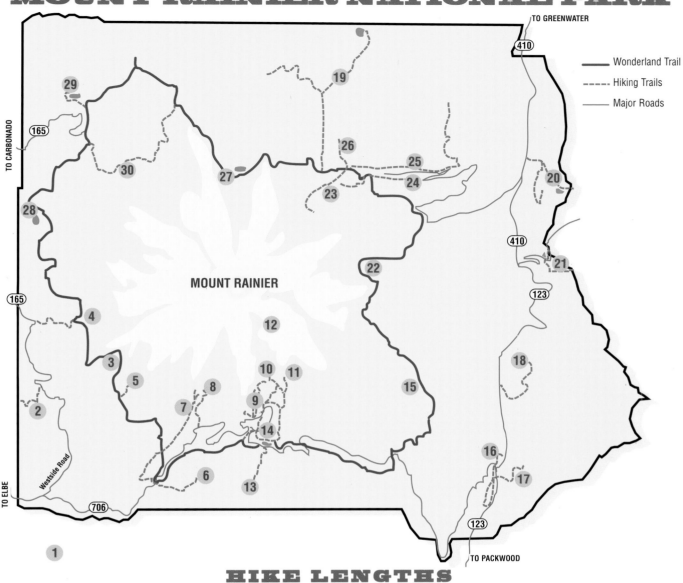

HIKE LENGTHS

1-5 miles

		Round Trip	Total Elev.
1.	High Rock	3 mi.	1300 ft.
9.	Paradise Trails	1-3 mi.	500 ft.
10.	Panorama Point	5 mi.	1400 ft.
11.	Paradise Glacier	5 mi.	1200 ft.
13.	Plummer Peak	3.2 mi.	1500 ft.
14.	Reflection Lakes	2.9 mi.	500 ft.
16.	Grove of the Patriarchs	1.6 mi.	0 ft.
17.	Silver Falls	3 mi.	300 ft.
21.	Naches Peak	4.5 mi.	700 ft.
24.	Yakima Park	2.4 mi.	200 ft.
25.	Dege Peak	3.4 mi.	900 ft.

6-10 miles

2.	Gobblers Knob	9.4 mi.	1500 ft.
3.	Emerald Ridge	7.7 mi.	2400 ft.
6.	Eagle Peak	7 mi.	3000 ft.
7.	Rampart Ridge	7.4 mi.	3000 ft.
8.	Van Trump Park	6 mi.	2200 ft.
12.	Camp Muir	9 mi.	4600 ft.
18.	Shriner Peak	8.4 mi.	3400 ft.
19.	Grand Park	6 mi.	1200 ft.
20.	Crystal Lakes	6 mi.	2300 ft.
22.	Summerland	8.4 mi.	2000 ft.
26.	Mt. Fremont Lookout	6 mi.	1000 ft.
29.	Tolmie Peak	7 mi.	1400 ft.
30.	Spray Park	6 mi.	2100 ft.

11-20 miles

4.	Klapatche Park	2.6 mi.	3900 ft.
5.	Indian Henry's Hunting Ground	11 mi.	2500 ft.
15.	Cowlitz Divide	15 mi.	4400 ft.
23.	Burroughs Mountain	11.3 mi.	3000 ft.
27.	Mystic Lake	14.6 mi.	3800 ft.
28.	Golden Lakes	20 mi.	3500 ft.

INTRODUCTION

This is a pictorial hiking book about one of the Northwest's prominent landmarks: 14,410-foot glacier-clad Mount Rainier. Many of our Northwest peaks do not retain their native names and Mount Rainier (named for a rear admiral of Captain George Vancouver's) is no exception. Tahoma was the generic Indian term for "snow peak" and specifically was named "Tah-ko-bah" by the Puyallup Indians, "Tah-ho-mah" by the Nisquallys and "Ta-ko-bet" by the Duwamish. Local mountain men referred to the peak as "Old He". By any name the mountain dominates the Washington skyline from Olympia to Everett. From the summit of Mount Baker on a clear day, this higher volcano to the south is visible well over 100 miles away.

The national park was established on March 2, 1899 and celebrates its centennial anniversary this year. Mount Rainier National Park ranks as one of our country's oldest parks along with Yosemite and Yellowstone. In 1915 Stanford University professor Bailey Willis wrote:

I have seen the glories of Switzerland, the grandeur of the Andes, and the grace of the beautiful cone of Fujiyama, but among the most renowned scenery of the world, I know of nothing more majestic or more inspiring than the grandeur of my own old camping ground, Mount Rainier.

This book includes hike descriptions and what I experienced while doing them, some of the park's natural history, and my tips on how to get good photographs. There is a list of recommended books in the back of the text for more information. The following six maps are best suited for the mountain: Green Trails Maps: Mt. Rainier West #269 and East #270, Packwood #302 and USGS 7 1/2" Mowich Lake, Sunrise, Mt. Rainier West and East.

Most of the hikes are within Mount Rainier National Park, although several hikes begin outside the park and one hike is completely out of the park. Since the majority of Mount Rainier's visitors enter the park from the southwest on the Longmire-Paradise Highway 706, I have organized the hikes beginning just west of the Nisqually entrance and proceeding counterclockwise around the mountain. In several instances hikes share the same approaches and I have consolidated this information to cut down on redundancy.

Mountain bikes are handy but not mandatory for four of the hikes listed. It is a lot more enjoyable and quicker to access Emerald Ridge and Klapatche Park via biking up the west side road (currently closed to auto traffic). Also, bikes enable one to create a couple of nice loop hikes on Rampart Ridge and Dege Peak by stashing a bike at the other end of the hike and coasting back down the road to your car.

Hiking times are not listed in this book. People need to look at the hike length, elevation gain, their conditioning and how much they are carrying to estimate a hiking time. From experience individuals will learn how long a hike will take them.

Access and Season

Access to the trails described in this book may change depending on road and trail washouts and construction. I discovered one cannot always rely on the park service's recorded road closure information. Again, a mountain bike can be useful for traveling roads closed to vehicles, especially if there is not a lot of elevation gain. Between 1976 and 1998 I hiked all 215 miles of trails listed here, two thirds of this during 1998. Hopefully, you won't find too many surprises, but do check on current conditions.

Mount Rainier National Park
　Tahoma Woods, Star Route
　　Ashford, WA 98304 . . . . . 360/569-2211
　Longmire . . . . 360/569-2211 ext. 3314
　Carbon River 360/829-5127
　Paradise . . . . 360/569-2211 ext. 2315
　White River 360/663-2273

The seasonal snowpack determines when one can access roads to various trails and when the trails are free of snow for easy hiking.

Low-elevation hikes (2,000 feet or lower) are generally hikable from May to November and the high-elevation hikes from late June to October depending on the seasonal snowpack and the first autumn storms. Highways and roads on the northwest, northeast and southeast sides of the park are closed throughout the winter.

Weather and Clothing

The Northwest receives a high level of precipitation (the average snowfall at Paradise is 630 inches in a year). Coupled with elevation and latitude, this more or less maintains Rainier's 26 glaciers that comprise 35 square miles of ice. For the hiker or climber venturing onto or around the huge volcano, weather and how quickly it changes is a major consideration. Due to orographic lifting, moisture in the air rises and condenses rapidly as it hits the mountain, thus hammering slopes even at the timberline level with high winds and heavy precipitation.

Cotton shorts and shirt are fine garments for a brief hike in the hot sun with no clouds in sight. But much of the year the weather is not predictable. Synthetic layers will keep your body warm even when wet. When one's core body temperature drops from being cold and not enough fuel in it (food), it leads to hypothermia rapidly. A waterproof shell jacket and pants are best in rain. Breathable/waterproof garments are overrated and actually the "best" piece of rainwear is a small collapsible umbrella. It keeps all the water off your head and shoulders, plus it breathes. Of course on windy ridges one can do a Mary Poppins with your bumbershoot, so stay off the high exposed places during a storm.

Footwear

I recommend a comfortable trail shoe or lightweight boot for footwear. If the trail is snow-covered or one has a weak ankle from a recent injury, boots treated for water reppellency are preferable. Putting tape or moleskin on your heels or trouble spots is advisable before doing longer hikes and will spare you much grief later. Once your feet are sweaty you will have difficulty getting tape to stick. Clean, dry socks also help prevent blisters and it is wise to carry extras, especially for overnight trips.

Environment

As humans we are adventurous and curious and we cannot resist getting down on our hands and knees to smell a flower closely, examine the moss or venture off the path for a better view or photograph. However, if in so doing we damage what we are trying to experience, it is hardly worth it. One can step carefully by staying on rocks, snow or bare patches of dirt and avoid crushing plants. Leave what you see for others and ask yourself "what will become of my collection of rocks, crystals, cones and bones when I am dead and gone?"

Camp in designated areas according to park service regulations on your backcountry permit and do not build any fires. Also observe rules for sanitation (distance from streams, etc.) when in the backcountry.

Don't get too close to animals and frighten them away so that the next group of hikers fail to enjoy the experience. Last summer there was a herd of 22 mountain goats on the slopes below Mt. Fremont Lookout. Because we all kept our distance from the animals, several later groups of hikers were able to see the goats.

Extra Supplies and Water

Over the years there has been much discussion over what one should carry on a mountain hike. During August of 1998 I did the Cowlitz Divide Hike 15 as a trail run. It took me 4 hours and 40 minutes including water, snack and photo breaks. At the end of the run I returned to Box Canyon and my car where a Wonderland Trail backpacker asked what I had done. Seeing I had only a small fanny pack,

Mount Rainier and grassy meadow in Grand Park.

Climbers on Carbon Glacier below Liberty Ridge. (Do not venture onto a glacier without experience and the proper equipment.)

the backpacker then asked what I carried with me. Here is what my pack contained:

Water bottle: 1 quart

Spare clothing: a light coated rain jacket, hat & gloves

Food: several candy & granola bars plus espresso beans

First aid kit: ibuprofen and a roll of tape

Small knife

Sunglasses

Green Trails Map of the area

Butane lighter and toilet paper

Camera: Nikon FM2 with a 28-70 zoom

Headlamp: if the run had been longer (it was 15 miles)

I have climbed to the summit of the mountain on three occasions by various routes and attempted one the steeper routes in winter, so I have that extra experience in my repertoire when hiking. You should carry more for potentially bad weather, medical problems or extended trips. It is purely a judgment call on your part. You can be fit, rely on your skill and use your head in the outdoors and have a very enjoyable experience without carrying a lot of gear.

To eliminate parasites or silt from water, good quality filter pumps are advisable. Boiling your water until it comes to a good rolling boil is adequate to kill microscopic critters (boil it for 10 minutes and you won't be able to carry enough fuel).

Camera Gear and Film

Some of the photos in this book were taken in previous years with a Pentax 6x7 or a Linhof Technika 4x5. My feeling now is that new films are much sharper and reproduction technology much better. Consequently, the lighter 35mm format was my choice for the nearly two dozen additional hikes completed in 1998. I carried a Nikon F-5 with a 20mm, 28-70 zoom, 50mm and a 70-300mm zoom. I used a 105mm Micro Nikkor for close-up work and a variety of sturdy tripods. Lightweight, flimsy tripods are difficult to use and make for unsharp photos, especially with long lenses. A cable release and a camera body with a mirror-lock up mechanism to reduce vibration when shooting are also essential.

Filters can be very useful for outdoor photography. The filters I used for images in this book were a Nikon A-2 or the slightly warmer Tiffen 812. Both will enhance the scene slightly to span the gap between what your eye and mind remembers and what the film records. This avoids the exclamation, "Gee I thought that sunset was a lot more vibrant!" I also used a standard polarizer to darken the sky, increase contrast with clouds or enrich colors. The Tiffen warm polarizer enables one to polarize and warm a scene simultaneously. In addition a graduated split density filter is useful for scenes with a lot of contrast between dark and light. Color films cannot record a bright snowy mountain in the background and a dark lake in the foreground without one element of the composition being too dark or too light. The split filter holds back light from the brightest area, allowing the photographer to achieve good results.

For hand-held photos, I used Fujichrome Sensia 100 exclusively and for tripod work Fujichrome Velvia 50 rated at ASA 32 (ISO is the current film speed abbreviation on the box and is the same as ASA). If you shoot Velvia at ASA 50 as it says on the box, it will turn out very dark. For night shots of star trails and peaks I sometimes use Ectachrome Professional Plus, EPP 100. This film does not turn green (as some films do) during long exposures necessary for photographing the night sky.

Final Thoughts

The summer of 1998 I was able to rediscover Mount Rainier by hiking to many beautiful places around the mountain. I did about half the hikes by myself, a half dozen with my Mom (who turned 75 that year) and the remaining ones with friends. During those trips I experienced lush flower meadows, verdant slopes, chirping and squeaking animals, mornings of lingering fog and a couple of wet and even snowy days. There was very little stormy weather that summer and I did not experience any difficulties.

Whether you are on your own or with friends there are still a myriad of hazards that might occur. Don't be packing a cell phone along with the idea of yelling for help at the slightest problem. You are responsible for your own actions and life-saving assistance is not readily available. There are only a few places on the mountain that cell phones actually work.

Be fit, be smart, take along what is necessary and get good photos to show your family and friends. Or keep a journal as many people do and describe your experiences through words. Edward Abbey said that "a word is worth a thousand pictures." Before you go out there I'll leave you with a bit of my philosophy:

You cannot go through life waiting for miracles to happen, for some amazing thing to occur that makes you happy, rich well or content.
The "real" miracle of life is that people make those things happen, whatever they are.

They smile and continue to go on despite their position in life. And by doing this they inspire others who in turn "discover" their miracle.

The other miracle of life is that we as humans exist. We could have been an insect, blade of grass or lump of dirt.
And since we have existed we have wreaked much havoc upon our only home and each other.
But we are the only species on this planet with the ability to affect change.

As one of five billion, it seems a staggering impossibility, but it can be done.

Star trails and climbers' lights leaving Camp Muir for a summit climb.

1 HIGH ROCK

Round Trip: 3 miles

Elevation Gain: 1300 feet

(Total Climbing)

High Rock Lookout is 13 air miles southwest of Mt. Rainier's summit and outside the national park. It provides an unusual vantage point to view the great volcano and its neighbors Mt. Adams and Mt. St. Helens.

Approaching Mt. Rainier Park eastbound on Hwy. 706 drive 10 miles from the junction of Hwy. 7 and 706 (Elbe) and turn right (south) on Forest Service Road 52. Follow Rd. 52 for 4.8 miles and turn right on Rd. 84 (brown High Rock Lookout sign), keep left at 2.5 miles and follow Rd. 84 for 11.6 miles. At Rd. 8440 turn right and drive 2.5 miles to Towhead Gap and the trailhead.

It was a hot day in late July when my mom and I chose to hike to the fire lookout. Mom had spent seven summers on a fire lookout southwest of Mt. St. Helens when I was a teenager. I was with her for six of those summers and ever since she has been keen to hike to and correspond with fire lookouts and their personnel all over Washington State.

The dusty trail followed a ridge up through hemlocks and beargrass with occasional glimpses of Rainier. Gigantic afternoon thunderheads building over the mountain offered good opportunities for afternoon photographs with a polarizing filter. Polarizers work best when light strikes the subject from the side at 90 degrees or so. The filters are constructed to cut scattered light. When used properly, they intensify colors and dramatize sky scenes, especially those with clouds. The filters are ineffective when the sun is behind, or in front, of the subject, so don't leave the filter on your lens all day long since it makes for darker viewing, difficult focusing and slower shutter speeds.

We finally reached the 5,685-foot lookout late in the day along with a half dozen other hikers. Bud Panco had worked at the lookout for the past 12 years for the Gifford Pinchot National Forest and remembered that mom had written to him several years before. Although the Northwest is not known for lightning activity, Bud described a storm several years before where he was up all night and counted over 100 lightning strikes on the surrounding hills and peaks. But that day in July, the boiling clouds stabilized and we were treated to views of the Tatoosh Peaks, Goat Rocks and the many serpentine glaciers flowing off Rainier.

Beargrass blooming along the trail to High Rock.

Opposite page: An afternoon descent from High Rock Lookout.

Mount Rainier and building thunderheads from the trail to High Rock.

2 GOBBLERS KNOB

Round Trip: 9.4 miles

Elevation Gain: 1500 feet

From the 5,485-foot Gobblers Knob Fire Lookout one views the massive west side of Mt. Rainier including Sunset Ridge, the 4.5-mile long Tahoma Glacier and Success Cleaver.

Approach as for Hike 1 and drive Hwy. 706 10.8 miles and turn left (north) on F.S. Rd. 59. Follow Rd. 59 for 8.5 miles past roads 37 and 79 to the end of maintained Rd. 59 and park. The trail to Glacier View and Gobblers Knob starts here. Follow the trail to a "T" and go right to Gobblers Knob. Contour around Mt. Beljica for 1.6 miles to junction with Lake Christine. Go left to Gobblers Knob and hike 2.4 miles past Goat Lake to the final junction below the knob. Go left and hike .7 miles to the lookout.

Mom and I did this hike together back in September of 1993. The weather was perfect and since it was a weekday we had the trail all to ourselves. Huckleberries carpeted the slopes bright red along the sides of the final path and clumps of mountain heather filled the niches in the rocks.

When we reached the lookout and ate some lunch (thankfully mom hadn't packed kipper snacks and rye crisp like on too many of our hikes when I was a kid), we had time to absorb the view of Rainier and many forested ridges in the foreground. I had been shooting Fujichrome Velvia film for the past two years and was pleased with the results later (Velvia provides richer colors all through the color spectrum and makes everything more vibrant). I did a lot of bracketing (over and underexposing) which gave me dark and light choices of the scenes I had shot once the film was processed.

We spent a leisurely afternoon at the top and started back to the car late. Dad was waiting in the camper and as mom began cooking dinner, I was able to shoot more film of evening light on the mountain and hazy valleys and ridges to the southwest. For the latter, scenes a medium-to-long lens (135mm, 180mm or 300mm) is best in order to pull in just the ridges and haze and not too much sky. I was using a 180mm on a sturdy tripod and the "dark card" method of exposing. This involves longer exposures (1 to 30 seconds) holding a dark card in front of the lens before the exposure, then tripping the shutter, taking away the card for the proper time and then replacing the card and letting the shutter close. In this way one completely eliminates vibration and soggy photos so common with long lenses. It also means that you have to stop the lens all the way down (in this case f 32) and even add a polarizer to cut the light and increase the length of exposure.

By the time the autumn light had faded I was done photographing and we all ate dinner as the first stars began to twinkle above the great peak.

Tahoma Glacier looms in sharp contrast behind the fireweed on Gobblers Knob.

Opposite page: Hiker and huckleberries on the trail to Gobblers Knob.

Hazy valleys and ridges in the magic light of evening.

3 EMERALD RIDGE

Round Trip: 7.7 miles + 7-mile bike

Elevation Gain: 2680 feet

As the name implies, the hiker ambles up through old growth forest to a ridge blanketed with grass and wildflowers below the Tahoma Glacier and Glacier Island.

One mile past the Nisqually entrance on Hwy. 706 (Paradise-Longmire Road), turn left (north) on the West Side Road and follow it 3 miles to where it's closed. Park here and mountain bike the road for 3.8 miles to Round Pass. Chain your bike to a tree out of sight and hike .8 of a mile down and (east) to the South Puyallup River Trail. Go right at the junction walking through old growth hemlock forest with numerous nursery logs containing baby seedlings. Tiny streams cleave the lush mossy forest floor and chunks of perfect hexagonal basalt columns lie like ancient ruins.

Follow the trail 1.1 miles to nearly the South Puyallup Camp and go right and 1.7 miles more up to Emerald Ridge: a high point along the 93 mile Wonderland Trail that encircles the mountain. Below and to the north the terminus of the Tahoma Glacier unloads tons of ground up rock where silt-laden streams carry the debris

Hemlock seedlings flourish on a nursery log.

down into the South Puyallup River and away to the west. If one could accelerate time it would be amazing to watch the big hill shrink in size from the carving action of the ice. Adventurous hikers can scramble up rock slabs another 400 feet for a closer look at another lobe of the glacier.

I did the hike in early August and found abundant meadows of lupine, paintbrush and buttercups. Owing to the mountain bike approach I chose to carry only two lenses that day, a 20mm extreme wide-angle and a 35-105mm zoom. The zoom was a Tamron brand and not a Nikkor and only worked well when used on a tripod. Regardless of the brand be careful about using slower shutter speeds when doing hand-held shooting, especially with even short tele-photos such as a 105mm. Using a shutter speed that is too slow creates unsharp photos due to camera shake. I generally double the recommended shutter speed of 125th for a 50mm lens up to a 250th and much faster for teles, 1000 and 2000th of a second. For the best results carry a good tripod.

The day was perfect,

Hexagonal basalt columns lie like ancient ruins deep in the forest.

I got plenty of exercise, good photos and had a fun 13-minute coast back down the road that had taken 45 minutes to cycle up.

A lush wildflower meadow high on Emerald Ridge.

*There are mountains, valleys and rivers winding free
carrying silt and pebbles down to the sea.
And someday when we are long gone,
those great peaks and deep canyons
will be smooth as a bone.*

*Opposite page:
Wonderland Trail backpackers taking a lunch break on Emerald Ridge.*

4 KLAPATCHE PARK

Round Trip: 12.6 miles + 7-mile bike

Elevation Gain: 3900 feet

This hike makes a good overnight trip to meadows below the Puyallup Glacier and Tokaloo Rock. During July and August there are sure to be lots of wildflowers and possibly goats anytime.

The approach is the same as for Emerald Ridge Hike 3. Panniers on the mountain bike are useful for getting some of the load off your back and onto the bike for the ride up to Round Pass. Just before the South Puyallup Camp go left and hike 4.4 miles and 1800 feet up to St. Andrews Park and back down 300 feet to Klapatche Park along the Wonderland Trail.

I backpacked to the park in 1976 on an attempt to climb the Sunset Amphitheater headwall on Rainier. The West Side Road was open then and the approach was much shorter. I was with a friend at the time and we had climbing gear and food for two days. We hiked through the park where avalanche lilies dotted the slopes white and above sun-cupped snow led up onto the Puyallup Glacier.

First bloomers after the spring snow melt, avalanche lilies at Klapatche Park below Puyallup Cleaver.

High on the Puyallup Cleaver at 11,000 feet a herd of 15 mountain goats were playing on the steep snowslopes. There wasn't a thing for them to eat up on the snow and they were literally just sliding down and climbing back up. It looked like snow school for the kids, of which there were several.

I had only three lenses with me: a 24mm wide-angle, a 50mm and a 105mm short tele. Of course I wanted the goats to show up much bigger in my photos and it's always a hard choice deciding how much camera gear to carry on an outdoor adventure. Generally when I am trying to do a climb I simply can't carry it all due to the

weight of the additional climbing equipment. My favorite choice now for a lightweight and versatile setup is: a 28-70mm 3.5/4.5 zoom and a 135mm 2.8 tele. I have a one pound table tripod that is useful for getting shots that require slow shutter speeds or for long night photos of the sky.

Conditions for our climb were much too warm and after watching rocks flying down the face, we opted to hike back down to the meadows and enjoy the flowers. Later that summer I tried to climb Liberty Ridge on the mountain's north side and also found the conditions too warm. It seemed as though it was a good year for hiking and just enjoying the sights.

Sunset from the camp on Puyallup Cleaver above Klapatche Park.

5 INDIAN HENRY'S HUNTING GROUND

Round Trip: 11 miles

Elevation Gain: 3200 feet

Indian Henry's (named for a Cowlitz Indian who hunted goats in the 1870s) is a collection of beautiful meadows at over 5,000 feet, with the Tahoma, Pyramid, Success and Kautz glaciers mantling the mountain above. It is a great place to do an overnight trip, although the nearest campsite is one mile east on the Wonderland Trail. In the height of the summer and on a weekend, getting a backcountry permit might be difficult. I have been into the area twice on day hikes and wished I had had more time.

Approach via the Kautz Creek Trail by continuing east on Highway 706 3.2 miles beyond the Nisqually entrance to the park and park on the right. The trail begins on the north side of the road and climbs 3200 feet around the east side of Mt. Ararat, then drops

Alpenglow on Success Cleaver from Indian Henry's Hunting Ground in autumn.

100 feet into Indian Henry's. To reach Mirror Lakes one mile further, go left at the junction with the Wonderland Trail and right at the next junction in .3 mile.

The first time into the hunting ground for me was in August of 1992 and I carried a four-pound Fuji 6x9cm rangefinder camera and a tripod. The 65mm lens is wide and roughly equivalent to a 28mm on a Nikon. I was hoping for shots of meadows packed with flowers and the mountain behind but I was thwarted by an unexpected adversary: mosquitoes! In fact they were so thick that I had to wave them off the front of the lens before making an exposure. Normally I would have spent more time and explored the meadows for the best patch of flowers and then shot a lot of film from different perspectives, but not that day. Had I done an overnight trip the little beasties would have been less active in the cool morning or late evening when the light is much better anyway.

The second trip in was with a friend during October of 1996 and following a dusting of autumn snow. I carried a Linhof Technika 4x5 and the Fuji 6x9 loaded with Velvia, hoping to get nice light on the mountain from Mirror Lake. We did have good color on the slopes even though the snow had melted off the sub-alpine firs in the previous sunny days. I used the Fuji 6x9 for shots of my friend hiking and outfitted him with a bright yellow pullover (see pages 2-3).

We did shoot the last light on the peak and then stumbled out the snowy trail with headlamps, reaching the car well after dark. There were however, absolutely no mosquitoes.

Above and below: Lupine abounds in the meadows of Indian Henry's Hunting Grounds.

6 EAGLE PEAK

Round Trip: 7 miles

Elevation Gain: 3000 feet

Eagle Peak saddle at 5800 feet and Chutla Peak to the southeast some 200 feet higher, offer fantastic views of Rainier's southern slopes, the Tatoosh Peaks (including Pinnacle, Castle and Plummer) and Mt. Adams and St. Helens to the south. In addition, beargrass and other wildflowers grace the final steep meadows below the saddle in mid-summer.

Drive from the Nisqually entrance 6.3 miles to Longmire then turn right just before the ranger station. Park near the community house. Walk northeast to the suspension bridge and then 200 feet more to the trailhead on the left. The lower portion of the trail climbs through an old hemlock forest with a mossy floor. It stays in the woods for 3 miles or so and then ascends steeply for the last half mile to the saddle.

Once at the saddle one can scramble up a steep climber's path (some class 3 and 4) to Chutla Peak at 6000 feet and even better views. If you're not comfortable on bits of brushy exposed rock, better stay at the saddle. At the top of Chutla Peak one looks down into a beautiful glacial cirque on the north side of Wahpenayo Peak. Steep streams drop down through velvety meadows and into jagged talus fields.

I was tempted to shoot more images of distant volcanoes with a long lens but changed my mind. In the afternoon there can be a lot

Mount Adams on a crystal-clear day from Chutla Peak.

Wahpenayo Peak above a glacier-carved cirque from Chutla Peak.

of atmospheric haze (or pollution depending on where you are) and a telephoto lens compresses the perspective and amplifies haze and smog. It's better to shoot distant scenes in the cool of morning or evening when there are less heat waves as well. A polarizing filter can also help cut through some of it.

I did the hike in the summer of 1998 after having done another hike earlier in the day. I was fairly tired and lounged about on the summit snacking and absorbing the surroundings. The mountains seemingly last forever, although technically this is not true since they eventually erode away from glacial action and weathering. As humans our time on the planet is indeed brief and I reflected upon where our molecules might wind up.

There is a place where we will all go,
but to tell the truth, where it is, I don't know.

If I had any say about it,
it would be on top of a craggy summit.

Where wind and snow would blow my bits,
down into those icy pits.

And there the glacier would munch and grind,
and of me there would be nothing left behind.

Beargrass along trail ascending to Eagle Peak.

7 RAMPART RIDGE

Round Trip: 7.4 miles + 4.7-mile bike

Elevation Gain: 3000 feet

Rampart Ridge offers beautiful hiking through hemlock forest that leads to open meadows up to Mildred Point and spectacular flower displays and vistas.

From the Nisqually entrance drive Hwy. 706 6.6 miles and past Longmire to where the Wonderland Trail crosses the highway. Begin Rampart Ridge hike here or, if you want to make a loop out of it, drive another 3.6 miles to the Comet Falls trailhead, ditch and lock your bike in the woods and return back down the road to the start of the hike. Follow the Wonderland Trail for 1.6 miles and go right on the Rampart Ridge Trail. In 2.2 miles more go left and hike another .5 miles up to Mildred Point. From Mildred Point, backtrack to the last junction and go left to Van Trump Park, then down to Comet Falls and your hidden bike. Bike 3.6 miles back to your car or retrace your original route up for a round trip hike of 8.6 miles.

The trail begins steeply, gaining 1600 feet of elevation in the first two miles and remains in the woods for a total of 3.5 miles. The last bit up to Mildred Point is a very steep unmaintained path that passes incredible flower meadows during July and August. From the top at 5,935 feet one gets great views of Mt. Adams, the Tatoosh Range and Van Trump Park just to the east. Northward, the Kautz Glacier discharges rubble and several muddy waterfalls carry away the finer rock flour ground up by the moving ice.

If making a loop hike out of it, one crosses Van Trump Creek just below the Park, that in 1998 had a beautiful display of purple monkey flowers and intensely vibrant green moss.

The best light for shooting nature scenes and close-ups is an overcast day where there are no shadows and very low contrast. The scattered light from the sky evenly illuminates every part of the subject you are shooting and the colors are rich and soft. Photographing the same scene in bright sunlight creates harsh shadows and colors and poor illumination.

A solid tripod and a lens that stops down to f 22 or 32 to obtain good depth of field is mandatory. A macro lens is useful for getting really close, but if there is any wind you will have a long wait for it to die down or you may need to carry along a hinged Plexiglas contraption to shield the flower on three sides from the breeze while shooting.

I did the hike and bike during August and found ski poles useful in crossing Van Trump Creek as there is no bridge. Mountain streams may be impassable at the peak snowmelt earlier in the summer and it may be better to simply turn around and go back the way you came rather than risk a serious accident. As it was August, the water was low and I hopped boulders, then spent an hour shooting the flowers and moss.

Finally, having exhausted my film and the patience of the blossoms (I think they asked the wind to shoo me away), I made my way down past Comet Falls, talus slopes and lower Van Trump Creek to my hidden bike. Once in the saddle it was a thrilling 10 minute ride back to the car.

Opposite page:
Monkey flowers and velvety moss thrive along a side-channel of Van Trump Creek.

Lupine meadow below Mildred Point and the Tatoosh Peaks visible in the distance.

8 VAN TRUMP PARK

Round Trip: 6 miles

Elevation Gain: 2200 feet

This hike is not too long and passes spectacular Comet Falls enroute to the meadows of Van Trump Park above. Keep an eye out for pikas and their small "hay piles" in the talus fields down low.

Approach as for Rampart Ridge and drive Hwy. 706 another 3.6 miles to the Comet Falls trailhead just before the Christine Falls bridge. Climb steadily for 2.5 miles past Comet Falls and up many switchbacks to the beginning of Van Trump Park. Go right at the junction and hike up another .5 miles and several hundred feet to good views and open meadows.

My mom and I did this hike in August of 1992 on a fine day with swirling clouds drifting about the sky (and squadrons of mosquitoes on patrol). I was carrying my Fuji 6x9 and a Leitz tripod and was amazed that I got any photos at all in the adverse conditions we experienced with the winged creatures. However, as we gained a bit more altitude we encountered some breeze which helped to disperse them. As the clouds came and went we could get glimpses of the Kautz and Wapowety Cleavers and the small Van Trump Glaciers.

It is difficult to capture good landscape images when your subject has direct midday light on it. My favorite lighting is early morning and late evening when the sun strikes objects from the side at a low angle. One should also be careful not to include any sky when composing landscape photos on overcast days, since your eye will immediately be drawn upward to the blank gray area with nothing in it. One exception might be if the clouds have some shape to them as happens during a storm or a bit of color. But it is wiser to point your lens down on overcast days and take advantage of the indirect lighting to illuminate nature's living things on the ground.

After a quick snack, I shot several images of the peak with flowers or rocks in the foreground to give depth to the scene. We then started back down listening for the squeaks of pikas and stepping carefully on the rocky sections of trail.

Opposite page: Hemlock, cedars and alder cloak the mossy walls of Comet Creek.

Below: Moss campion, paintbrush and lupine carpet the meadows of Van Trump Park below Mt. Rainier.

9 PARADISE TRAILS

Round Trip: 1 to 3 miles

Elevation Gain: 500 feet

Of all the remote and beautiful places to observe flower displays on Mt. Rainier one can often find the best flowers very near Paradise. From mid-July to mid-August (depending on the season) there is a great mix of species blooming including glacier and avalanche lilies, lupine, paintbrush, gentian, asters and purple monkey flowers.

There are a couple of popular trails to Nisqually Vista and Alta

Lupine meadows in the evening near Paradise.

backlighting of flowers where they are glowing from behind. Foggy or overcast days can still be the best due to the even illumination and soft rich colors.

Some of my flower images around Paradise were shot with a Linhof Technika 4x5 inch camera. The depth of field (sharpness from foreground to background) is terrible which necessitates a very small lens opening (aperture) of f 32 or f 45 and the use of a sturdy tripod. Since the lens opening is small, the exposure time increases so that even in bright light you may be shooting at 1/4, 1/2 or 1 second. Any wind is disastrous. Of course you can try an impressionistic approach and let the wind blow the flowers from side to side creating blurs with some of the blossoms.

Paradise gets a lot of camera activity during the flower season so be extra careful about not stepping off the trail and squashing plants. Besides, your tripod will rest more solidly on the good asphalt paths that are provided. Whatever size camera you are using it is best to spend some extra time and wander about looking at different areas. Putting the camera on a tripod will cause you to slow down your shooting process and force you to observe more carefully what is going on in the composition. In turn you will learn more, appreciate more and hence relate what you experienced more evocatively to others.

Vista that provide glacier and mountain views. In the autumn the flowers give way to brilliant red slopes of mountain ash and huckleberry.

Follow Hwy. 706 (Longmire-Paradise Road) 17.4 miles from the Nisqually park entrance to Paradise. The Nisqually Vista trail begins from the end of the west parking lot near the visitor center and the Alta Vista trail from the north edge of the Paradise parking lot.

The key to the best flower displays is learning from others when the "peak" of the show is. The park service receives many calls from people asking this very question and it is best to talk to other photographers. When there is a good flower year one finds a variety of blossoms carpeting the slopes in profusion. Then the trick is to get good light and no wind, not an easy task. Early morning is sometimes the best for no wind, especially when the flowers are still heavily laden with dew. The warm evening light is also good for

Life can become a blur.
If we are not careful it moves too fast.
Slow down, look around, take your time, feel the ground.
Watch the dewdrop glisten and fall to the earth.
Speak not a word and smell the air up high.
These are the things that we should all try.
Build no more bombs or huge factories.
Take a quiet walk amid the tall trees.

Opposite page: Lupine, paintbrush and asters in early morning.

10 PANORAMA POINT

Round Trip: 5 miles
Elevation Gain: 1400 feet

In the Paradise area, Panorama Point offers a medium-length hike to a high vista with the Tatoosh Range, Goat Rocks, Mt. Adams and Mt. St. Helens to the south. During flower season (in late summer) there are many species blooming along the way. During a peak year rolling slopes of buttercups, lupine, paintbrush and avalanche lilies provide a colorful foreground to the mountain backdrop.

Approach as for Hike 9 and start walking behind the inn on the north edge of the parking lot. Go right (east) and take the trail to Alta Vista, (Myrtle Falls on NPS signs) and Golden Gate Falls going counterclockwise up to the point. Go left at Vista Falls at .5 miles and left again at Golden Gate Falls at 1.5 miles. There may be snow covering the trail as you approach Panorama Point, even in midsummer. Descend and go left on Skyline Trail for the return to Paradise.

I did the hike with my mom during late July of 1998 and we saw plenty of avalanche lilies and buttercups still blooming in the meadows along Edith Creek. There seemed to a be a constant breeze blowing so I didn't use a tripod all day, since it would have been frustrating waiting for the flowers to stop quivering. I used a polarizing filter most of the time on a 35-105mm zoom with the lens at 35mm. It is tricky getting a polarizer to work on lenses wider than 35mm as the filter will darken the corners of the image (vignetting) and spoil your shot. If one can find a company that makes thin polarizers, they can be used on 28mm and 24mm wide-angle lenses.

After pausing often to shoot images of the flower fields, we finally took a snack break above Panorama Point where the green slopes of the lower mountain swept gently down to Paradise. In the background the Tatoosh Peaks of Unicorn, Castle, Pinnacle and Plummer formed a jagged dark barrier and Washington's southern volcanoes floated like clouds on the horizon.

We joined the scores of Saturday hikers up enjoying the mountain splendor. Once we integrated ourselves into the throng, we began paying more attention to their conversations than the scenery. Fashion, romance and medical problems seemed to be high on the list of topics on that sunny weekend on the mountain.

Hiker on one of the many paved trails near Paradise en route to Panorama Point.

11 PARADISE GLACIER

Round Trip: 5 miles

Elevation Gain: 1200 feet

This is a nice hike over to the remnants of Paradise Glacier with good views of Stevens Creek and Stevens Ridge. There are lush flower meadows in mid-summer and red huckleberry slopes in early autumn.

Begin the hike from Paradise as for Hike 10 and at .5 miles go right at Alta Vista Falls. Descend and cross Paradise Creek. Continue up and over Mazama Ridge and keep left at the junction to Reflection Lakes. In another .4 miles go right at the Stevens-Van Trump Memorial and hike another .5 miles to a rocky knoll above and east of the trail with a good view of McClure Rock, Paradise

Autumn slopes of huckleberry near Paradise Creek.

Glacier and Cowlitz Rocks. The open meadows of Mazama Ridge give way to rocky slopes to the north where glaciers carved the terrain in the past. Tiny streams meander through the talus fields and clumps of yellow mountain monkey flowers sprout from patches of bright green moss.

Paradise Glacier is an example of a secondary or "inter" glacier that is completely sustained by snowfall. It is a combination of two torpid bodies of ice that flank the 700,000 year-old volcano.

I did the hike in September with a friend and we found the slopes of huckleberries brilliant in the late afternoon. Shooting photographs of people hiking takes some forethought and cooperation from your companion. If there is a particular place you want the person to be in the composition it is best to give them specific

Hiker enjoying a view of Mt. Adams from below Paradise Glacier.

instructions. If the sun is behind the hiker he or she will be a black shadow and not show up. Front or side lighting works well,

especially if the light illuminates the person's face and clothing. Have the person keep walking instead of standing still. You may have to ask the person to repeat a short section of trail more than once to get the photo you want. The use of a polarizing filter enhances the rich reds of the huckleberry slopes and darkens the blue sky.

Boot tracks on the dusty trail.

From the end of the hike you can return the way you came or take a left at the hike's low point (Paradise Creek) and hike a path along the stream down to the highway. You can hitchhike or walk back up to Paradise parking lot or if you're with a friend, maybe they will hike back the long way and drive the car down to Paradise Creek.

Vibrant red clumps of knots newberry in autumn near Paradise Glacier.

12 CAMP MUIR

Round Trip: 9 miles

Elevation Gain: 4400 feet

At a height of 10,000 feet, Camp Muir is the high camp for many mountaineers attempting a climb of Mt. Rainier. Since the elevation is much greater than many peaks in the Cascades and the upper portion of the march is always snow-covered, it is a journey for experienced hikers only. The site was chosen by John Muir in 1888 during the fourth ascent of the mountain via the Gibralter Route and originally was called "Cloud Camp". The camp offers stunning views southward of Mt. Adams, Mt. St. Helens and the Tatoosh Range often rising above a sea of clouds.

Approach as for Hike 11 and from behind the Paradise Ranger Station take the Skyline Trail to the Pebble Creek Trail and the Muir Snowfield. Pass Alta Vista in .5 miles, Glacier Vista in 1.2 miles and Panorama Point in 2.5 miles. Above Pebble Creek the slope broadens and drops off steeply on the west to the Nisqually Glacier and to the Cowlitz Glacier on the east. It is no place to get caught in a whiteout or storm since the path is not always obvious or marked with wands. The Muir Snowfield can have crevasses especially where it borders the Nisqually and Cowlitz Glaciers. Although not steep, in slippery conditions one could slide out of control and get injured. An ice axe (and how to use it) is essential gear, as is a compass. The appropriate compass bearings are as follows: Pebble Creek to Moon Rocks, 328 degrees magnetic (reverse reading is 148 degrees) and Moon Rocks to Camp Muir, 322 degrees (reverse reading 142 degrees).

Don't be daunted by these warnings but use good judgment and pick decent weather when ascending to Camp Muir. Carry extra food and clothing and be ready to retreat when conditions turn bad. On a perfect day the rewards are great. I have been up to Camp Muir several times climbing and skiing and had an interesting and educational adventure back in May of 1985.

I was alone and had planned to meet up with friends in the evening at around 8,000 feet or so. They had started earlier with a tent, stove and overnight gear with the intention of hiking the rest of the way to Camp Muir the next day. I was going light with a sleeping bag, pad and minimal food and fluids. I didn't leave the parking lot until 7 p.m. and in just 30 minutes a thick fog rolled in as it began to snow. I continued up into the gloom not knowing precisely where they had camped or where I was. Finally it was too dark to keep going and as the wind had picked up, I bivouacked on the lee side of a boulder. Dinner consisted of a can of beer and sardines. I was soaked with sweat from skiing up with climbing skins on and quickly saturated my down bag

(a poor choice for that trip). I hadn't brought a bivy sac thinking I would be in a tent with them. It was a cold night, I did not sleep at all and in the morning my bag was covered with fresh snow.

The day dawned perfectly clear, so I started up toward Camp Muir. I met them on the way back down and enjoyed some of the finest spring skiing I have ever done. The slopes and surrounding peaks were crisp with new snow and by afternoon the sun was blazing hot. Luckily I experienced no injuries but had learned some valuable lessons: don't be pig-headed about continuing on in bad weather, don't be ill prepared and bring more food and fluids.

❧

Let the cold wind drone as I go alone,
up into the mountains and the snow.
Past the snowy ridges where there are no ledges,
and the thin air takes my breath away.
Don't look down you witless clown,
ere the crowded city draws you back.
I could have stayed in bed, but now I've lost my head,
to the foggy peak up in the alpine realm.

❧

Opposite page: Mount Adams floats above a sea of clouds from a vantage point above Camp Muir.

Below: Ptarmigan in its winter plumage below Camp Muir.

13 PLUMMER PEAK

Round Trip: 3.2 miles
Elevation Gain: 1500 feet

A hike up to Pinnacle Peak Saddle, then west and up to 6,370 foot Plummer Peak provides one the opportunity to see fabulous flower meadows and unusual views of Mt. Rainier. One may be visited by deer, marmots, pikas and Gray Jays along the path to these two andesitic peaks of the Tatoosh Range. The rock is made up of mudflows and lavas that was prominent on other peaks in the park, before erosion and time did their work.

Paintbrush and lupine glow with evening light on the slopes of Plummer Peak.

From the Nisqually entrance, drive 15.4 miles on Hwy. 706 to the Paradise River crossing. Instead of going left up to Paradise, turn right and drive another 1.4 miles to Reflection Lakes and park. The trail to Plummer and Pinnacle peaks is across the road (south side) from the lake. The trail climbs steadily toward the saddle and may have a substantial amount of snow over the tread until late in the season. From the saddle it is another 400 feet to the top and the path is tricky with steep drop-offs on both sides. Be careful that the sheer sides of late season snowbanks do not force you onto slippery terrain.

Once in the highest meadows near the summit a profusion of varied flowers bloom when the time is right including: asters, bistort, paintbrush, lupine and louseworts. A couple of years ago I did the hike in July and found avalanche lilies lower down in addition to the above flowers.

I started the hike late, hoping to capture late evening light on the meadows and the mountain. On that trip I was using a Pentax 6x7cm with 45mm, 75mm, 105mm and 300mm lenses (equivalent to a 24mm, 35mm, 50mm and a 150mm on a Nikon). Since the depth of field (sharpness from foreground to background) is not good on medium format cameras one must use the smallest aperture possible and longer exposures. That means waiting for the breeze to stop blowing, especially frustrating if the evening light is fading fast. But sometimes late in the day is when the wind dies down and all those pretty little blossoms finally hold still.

A polarizing filter will improve the contrast between the sky and the mountain and enrich colors. If the light has a slight warm cast to it already, a warm polarizer might be a good choice of filters since it will polarize and warm up the scene slightly. That day in July the light was soft and rich. When it faded I scurried down to the saddle and put on my headlamp for the remaining descent through the woods to the car.

A profusion of avalanche lilies blanket the slopes of Plummer Peak.

14 REFLECTION LAKES LOOP

Round Trip: 2.9 miles

Elevation Gain: 500 feet

This is a beautiful loop hike with great views of Pinnacle Peak, Louise Lake and Mt. Rainier. The mountain is often mirrored in the calm waters of the lake, especially at dawn or in the late evening.

Approach as for Hike 13 (17.3 miles from the Nisqually entrance) and park in the turnout on the south side of the larger lake. Walk east and pick up the trail on the far edge of the smaller lake. Follow the trail counterclockwise going left at every trail junction. In .8 miles one can look down on the lakes and across to the Tatoosh Range from Faraway Rock. At 2 miles, one can take a side trip to the right (80 yards) for a good glimpse of Mt. Rainier. The hike is dotted by many small tarns nestled among subalpine firs and mountain hemlock. Follow the loop trail back down to the larger Reflection Lake and walk along the lake or a short stretch of road back to your car.

I did the hike in the autumn of 1998 with a friend and we started late as I wanted to catch the early morning light on the mountain first. While waiting I noticed two expired dragonflies laying next to each other and laden with dew. It made a good close-up subject using the 105mm Nikkor Micro lens. Since I was using the lens at f 32 for good depth of field, the exposures were long (10-30 seconds). The pair of bugs weren't going anywhere so blurring was not a problem. The light was however not the best. It was a clear day with the insects in the shade. This produced a blue cast to the color because of the clear sky above. I made a second batch of coffee on the truck tailgate and waited some more. Finally the sun crept over a nearby wooded ridge and lit up my two subjects for only a moment.

Their giant green eyes became iridescent and small drops of water on grass blades scintillated in the morning sunshine. Had I brought along the Nikon extension bellows for the lens, I would have gotten even closer and shot the beautiful lacework pattern in the dragonfly

Dragonflies laden with dew.

wings. As it was the coffee was cold and it was time to start our hike.

The temperature had warmed up and no one else was on the trail that day. Clumps of huckleberries had started turning red and patches of grass lay flat and heavy with dew from the night before. Near the end of the hike a doe and fawn grazed contentedly near the trail and seemed unalarmed by our presence. We finished the loop early and still had time for another short hike in the afternoon.

Dense forest mirrored in the waters of Reflection Lakes.

15 COWLITZ DIVIDE

Round Trip: 15 miles

Elevation Gain: 4400 feet

Cowlitz Divide to Indian Bar is a scenic hike along a high open ridge. To the west one looks across to Cowlitz Park, the Whitman, Fryingpan and Ohanapecosh glaciers. Also visible is 11,138-foot Little Tahoma, (a peak higher than many cascade summits) but only an erosional remnant of the once greater volcano. To the north are the dark spires of the Cowlitz Chimneys and Double Peak. The hike can be done as an overnight if one can get a backcountry permit from the park. It can also be done as a long day hike, or as I did it, a trail run of 4 and 1/2 hours.

Approach as for Hike 14 and continue east on the Stevens Canyon Road 24.3 miles from the Nisqually entrance to Box Canyon. Start the hike at Box Canyon and hike the Wonderland Trail past Nickel Creek Camp and up through a hemlock forest. Go left at junction in 2.8 miles and follow the Wonderland to Cowlitz Divide and Indian Bar. The trail climbs gradually for the most part with some steep sections up to 5900 feet (the high point on a grassy

Hikers in the Cowlitz Divide on a September afternoon.

ridge). The trail then drops 900 feet down to Indian Bar, crossing beautiful meadows and tiny streams.

At Indian Bar is a stone shelter (reportedly infested with mice) and the Ohanapecosh River draining the Ohanapecosh Glaciers above. Flowers are plentiful in the meadows during the peak season.

In September of 1998 I ran to Indian Bar and back on a hot day and carrying minimal gear. I chose to take only some extra clothing, snacks, water and of course a Nikon with a 28 - 70mm zoom lens. It was a long grind from Box Canyon up to the high point at 5900 feet, where I took a snack and water break. A group of four shirtless lads came storming up the trail from Indian Bar

Author dipping water from a stream at Indian Bar below the Cowlitz Divide.

on a day hike and asked me where I had camped. I said I was doing a trail run for the day for which I received puzzled and skeptical looks from them all.

Indian Bar was a long descent over 1.5 miles and I did not relish the 900 foot climb back out. I felt invigorated after a candy bar, some instant tea and a good stretch. On the way down to Indian Bar I passed the remains of lush lupine and heather meadows. At the Ohanapecosh River I took another good break and shot some images using a one pound table tripod propped on a boulder.

It was a long slow run up and over Cowlitz Divide and back down to Box Canyon. By the time I reached the parking lot it was time for

The brilliant, saturated hues of monkey flower blooms at Indian Bar.

ibuprofen, a beer from the cooler and chance to reflect on the sanity of such endeavors.

A long trail to this place, working, training and learning.
The path is so long, one step at a time is all it takes.
Forget not the beauty all around and the end in sight.

16 GROVE OF THE PATRIARCHS

Round Trip: 1.6 miles
Elevation Gain: None

Here is an opportunity to see 1,000-year-old Douglas firs, western red cedars and western hemlocks via a short flat walk through the forest and across the Ohanapecosh River.

Approach as for Hike 15 and drive the Stevens Canyon Road (east) 34 miles from the Nisqually Entrance. Park in large lot on left just .25 miles west of the Stevens Canyon Entrance. The trail begins in woods on the northeast side of parking lot and follows the Ohanapecosh River for .4 mile to a junction. Go right and cross bridge over river and in .2 of a mile reach the start of a loop trail through the big old trees.

There are good examples nursery logs, gnarled cedar roots encircling entire logs and giant trees (some 12-15 feet in diameter at the base). Naturalists believe that the island in the Ohanapecosh River where the trees are, has isolated them and protected them from forest fires for centuries, allowing the trees to grow so large.

My parents did the hike with me in the summer of 1998 on a clear warm day. Dad isn't fond of uphill hikes so this one fit the bill and we ambled along at a leisurely pace. An old growth forest floor is a beautiful place to get down on your hands and knees and look closely at what's going on with regard to growth and decay. Rotting logs and thick moss are the perfect medium for fungi and baby cedar and hemlock

The author's parents Ty and Marianna Kearney, below a pair of giant hemlocks.

seedlings to get started. The latter trees are "tolerant" species meaning they tolerate shade and begin growing where a Douglas fir (needing a lot of sunlight) would falter.

Here then is an ideal place, particularly on a cloudy day, to photograph close-ups of the life of the forest floor. The macro lens and a tripod with legs that splay out and gets the camera down low, are essential tools. In addition a cable release and a lot of patience are required, since the exposures will be very long to achieve what you want. On my last visit to these same woods it was a cloudy day and very late. I was using a wide-angle lens at f 22 to capture the forest floor and hemlocks in the background. Because I was shooting with Fujichrome Velvia rated at asa 32, the exposures ranged from one to three minutes!

But whether you are photographing the ancient trees or just admiring them, it is a mystical place to lose your thoughts or create some new ones.

Long ago two seeds were dropped in the earth side by side.
It did not rain or snow for a very long time
and the earth around the seeds became dry and cracked.
Finally, on a cold December day it snowed
and the flakes sifted down into the cracks.
The sun shone between the clouds and the snow melted.
After a week in the moist earth the seeds germinated.
They shot up through the soil and reached for the sky.
From a dry wasteland sprang new life.
The climate changed and water nurtured the new life.
In time it grew into a forest.
The forest thrived and survived a millennium of man.
Yet it is man who can still destroy all that came before.

17 SILVER FALLS

Round Trip: 3 miles

Elevation Gain: 300 feet

This is an easy loop hike to a beautiful falls on the Ohanapecosh River and a mossy hemlock forest along the river. The woods and river scenes more than compensate for the absence of Mt. Rainier vistas.

Approach as for Hike 16 and continue east on Hwy. 706 for 34.3 miles to the junction of Hwy. 706 and 123. Turn right on Hwy. 123 and drive south for .3 mile and park on the right. The trail to Silver Falls starts on the right and descends to the Ohanapecosh River. In a short distance take a left at a "T" junction, and then a right at the next junction. Hike downhill and cross the bridge over the river and then another couple hundred yards to the falls overlook on the right. I thought the best views of the falls were just before crossing the bridge while still on the east side of the river.

Immediately after the falls overlook take a left and hike south toward Ohanapecosh Campground (going right takes one to the Stevens Canyon Entrance). Parallel the river on the west side for 1.1 miles to the campground and turn left to cross the paved bridge over the Ohanapecosh River. After crossing the bridge go left again to Silver Falls and hike .8 mile upstream on the east side to Laughingwater Creek. In .2 mile after the creek go right and in a short ways right again and uphill to your car.

During November of 1998 I hiked the loop on a Tuesday and had the path all to myself. I found the forest scenes very aesthetic and the falls roaring with ample water from the recent rains. There was a lot of white water flowing over the brink which does not always make for a good stream photo. Too much white in a color photo often draws

Open hemlock forests surround the tidy path to Silver Falls.

the eye quickly to it as does a bright sun in a blue sky. It is better to use a wide-angle lens and reduce the size of the falls and include more moss or trees in the foreground. Another approach is to shoot stream scenes where there are several small columns of water flowing over rocks or moss. In this way you include more color in the composition and not too much white water.

After shooting the falls I continued south toward the campground and discovered many opportunities to explore the mossy forest floor and the various plant life sprouting up.

18 SHRINER PEAK

Round Trip: 8.4 miles

Elevation Gain: 3400 feet

Shriner Peak offers great views of Mt. Rainier's eastern slopes, the Cowlitz Chimneys and the William O. Douglas Wilderness to the east. Because the trail begins at 2400 feet and ends at 5800 feet, a hiker passes through three life zones: the mountain forest (2,000-3,500 feet), the sub-alpine forest (3,500-5,000 feet) and the alpine forest (5,000 feet and higher).

Approach as for Hike 17 and turn left off the Stevens Canyon Road onto Hwy. 123 and drive north another 3.5 miles towards Cayuse Pass (37.8 miles from the Nisqually Entrance). Drive a short ways past the trailhead on the right and park in a large gravel strip on the left. The trail begins on the east side of the road and climbs steadily for 3400 feet with no turns or junctions to the top and the fire lookout. I did the hike with my

Mount Rainier and Cowlitz Chimneys from the catwalk of Shriner Peak Lookout.

mom in early September of 1998 and I will let her describe that fine day we had together in the mountains.

The sign read: "it's a long, hot way up to Shriner Peak." Quite an order for someone who'd been doing easy hikes all summer. With few switch-backs, the lower trail thread-ed its way among tall Douglas firs, cedars and hemlocks. For aways it paralleled Panther Creek, being well above it. Bordered by the lush foliage of thimbleberries, the trail soon emerged into the hot sun. I looked for wildflowers but they were scarce this late—a few asters, fireweed, pearly everlasting, the yellow of groundsel, an occasional paintbrush or a hardy blue-violet harebell. With no rain in August, the trail had become powdery with dust. Snowbrush thrust up dark

An Oregon grape leaf on the mossy floor of a hemlock forest.

Hiker descending Shriner Peak.

green lacquered leaves, each leaf tipped at an angle to the sun, an adaptation to the hottest days. The softness of grassy slopes were broken by masses of hellabore with their parallel-veined coarse leaves streaked with warm yellow, greens and browns.

Half-way up we were treated to our first view of the east side of Mt. Rainier—its dazzling whiteness spectacular against a blue wash of sky. Eventually the trail dropped into a high basin and we began ascending the final dome with no hint as to where the lookout might be. Vine maples afforded a splash of scarlet, maroon and crimson here and there; mountain ash was showing brilliant orange berries and there were a few blueberries to feast upon, too.

After many hours of plodding upward, the trail became very rocky and climbed in a northerly direction. Finally the lookout came in sight—it could be seen for only the last 1/4 mile or so. We were soon walking across a grassy knoll and climbing the two-story tower to its catwalk at 5,834 feet. Built in 1932, it is a weathered brown structure with a pyramid roof. The lower story was built for storage—the upper part a glass house for living that contained the firefinder, bed, gas stove and table.

Enjoying our lunch on the catwalk we marveled at the stupendous views of the giant of the Cascades—Tahoma or Mt. Rainier. Radiating from the volcano we could see the Cowlitz Divide, the Cowlitz Chimneys and Sourdough Ridge. Though the lookout is in Mt. Rainier National Park, bordering it on the east is the William O. Douglas Wilderness Area with its jumble of peaks. Far to the south we could see Mt. Adams, the Goat Rocks, the Dark Divide and Mt. St. Helens.

We had taken four hours and twenty minutes for the ascent; it took two hours and twenty minutes for the descent. For me the hike up there had meant many rests—thanks to Alan's patience I made it. Hiking to a lookout with such a view is a glorious experience. But I did not envy the firewatcher's arduous hike up to his summer home, especially with a load of supplies.

Mountain ash in the afternoon light along the Shriner Peak Trail.

19 GRAND PARK

Round Trip: 6 miles

Elevation Gain: 1200 feet

Grand Park offers fantastic views of Mt. Rainier from the northeast in a Wyoming-like setting. It is also possible to hear elk bugling in the fall and see mountain goats on the north slopes of Mt. Fremont. The approach described below begins outside of Mt. Rainier National Park. You will need to get a backcountry permit from the park if you plan to camp overnight in Berkeley Park or Lake Eleanor, enroute to Grand Park.

Dawn light glows off the icy surface of a pond in Grand Park.

Approach Grand Park from Enumclaw on Hwy. 410 and drive 18 miles to the small town of Greenwater. Road mileage's begin in Greenwater. From Greenwater continue for 6.3 miles on Hwy. 410 to Forest Service Road 73. Turn right (west) on F.S. Rd. 73 and follow it for 11.4 miles. Keep left at .5 miles, right at .6 miles, right at 1.3 miles, left at 1.8 miles, cross Huckleberry Creek at 5.6 miles, keep right at 8.3 miles, keep left at 8.7 miles and finally cross Eleanor Creek at 11.4 miles and park on right.

From the east side of Eleanor Creek follow an unmaintained path for nearly a mile to Eleanor Lake, gaining 600 feet. From the east end of the lake a maintained National Park trail begins and climbs another 600 feet in two miles to Grand Park.

I had hiked into Grand Park in 1992 the long way from Sunrise and had heard of the shorter approach from the north and Lake Eleanor. A friend and I hiked in from the lake in October of 1998 during superb weather and following a light dusting of snow on the mountain. My friend was also a professional photographer, so we were keen to spend the night out near the park and then catch the morning light on the mountain. We were not disappointed.

The trip in was pleasant as the path wove its way through an old hemlock forest and up toward Lake Eleanor: a small lake nestled in between ridges thick with conifers. A gang of gray jays seemed intent on badgering us out of any handouts we might offer them. I gave them a brief lecture on the merits of eating what nature has provided and sent them on their way.

We had the lake to ourselves and the temperature was very

pleasant for October. After a sound nights sleep we were up before dawn and hiked on into the park. We parked our tripods and cameras on the edge of a icy pond, where a few vestigial patches of snow remained from an earlier storm. The mountain looked spectacular.

I chose to use my 28 - 70mm Nikkor zoom lens and a graduated split density filter for the dawn light on the mountain. This filter holds back the brighter light in the sky and on the mountain but allows more light to reach the lens from the darker foreground. Later when the entire scene became brighter I used a regular polarizer and then a warm polarizer to shoot the pond and mountain. If one has time it is a good idea to shoot the scene with several focal lengths from wide-angle to short telephoto. This will give you some choices later when you get the film back from the lab.

Flame-red huckleberry leaves in the late autumn light of Grand Park.

Our time in Grand Park turned into one of those little trips into the mountains that you hate to see end. But even those of us who are self employed have obligations, hence we packed up our memories and exposed film and sauntered back down to the lake and the car.

I am in love with the air and the sky,
the trees and the rocks, the ice and the snow.
With mountains and lakes and rivers and streams.
I am happy to be alive and life is a dream.

20 CRYSTAL LAKES

Round Trip: 6 miles

Elevation Gain: 2300 feet

This is a pleasant hike up to a beautiful alpine lake at 5800 feet. There are views of Mt. Rainier, the Emmons Glacier and White River after one begins to clear the forest on the way up.

Approach as for Hike 19 and continue on Hwy. 410 until 18.6 miles from Greenwater. There is a large gravel parking lot at the State Highway Department maintenance sheds on the right. The trail to Crystal Lakes is on the left (east) side of the highway and begins very near Crystal Creek. The trail climbs steadily up through a hemlock forest to a junction at one mile. Go left here up to the lakes. The right hand trail is unmaintained and takes one up the west side of Crystal Peak (the rock is Breccia of the Ohanapecosh Formation) and an old fire lookout site.

The upper Crystal Lake is the prettier and larger of the two and sits in a cirque (a basin carved out by glacial action) surrounded by rocky peaks. Deer and sometimes elk frequent the open meadows around the lake. I did the hike in August of 1998 with a friend in the typical perfect weather of that summer.

Hiker on the path around Crystal Lakes.

Lightning storm at night.

On that day the sky was filled with wonderful puffy clouds and over Mt. Rainier thunderheads were building up as if someone were shooting the clouds from a giant can of shaving cream. Had we camped overnight up at the lakes there might have been better opportunities for lightning photographs, as I heard thunder that night from White River Campground. After dinner I did shoot several images of lightning in the sky from a nearby clearing.

Getting photos of lightning is especially difficult in the Northwest since we don't get many electrical storms on the west side of the Cascades or on the Cascade Crest. Should you find yourself in a safe position to shoot a lightning storm it is best to do it near sunset, dusk or at night. You will need slow speed film, a tripod, cable release and a lens with a large opening (f 2 or f 2.8 at least). Then the technique is to stop the lens down about two f stops (f 4 or f 5.6) and leave the shutter open a long time to allow several lightning strikes to be recorded on the film. It is useful to be very patient, have an umbrella handy (since there is usually a lot of rain with thunderstorms) and take notes on your experiments and exposure times.

Opposite page: Asters in bloom along the lake shore.
Below: Hiker enjoying the solitude of Crystal Lakes in late summer.

 **NACHES PEAK**

Round Trip: 4.5 miles

Elevation Gain: 700 feet

This is a pleasant hike near Chinook Pass and Tipsoo Lake that offers beautiful views of Dewey Lake to the southeast, nearby Mt. Seymour and the Tatoosh range farther south. In mid-summer, wildflowers are plentiful and in the autumn huckleberries color the slopes red.

Approach as for Hike 20 and continue on Hwy. 410 to Cayuse Pass (22.6 miles from Greenwater). Keep left and continue on Hwy.

410 another 4 miles to Chinook Pass and the National Park boundary above Tipsoo Lake. Just past the National Park sign there is a wide pullout on the right. The Naches Peak Trail starts here on east side of road. At this point one is actually hiking on the Pacific Crest Trail as it follows Naches Peak around its east side. One half of the trail is in the William O. Douglas Wilderness Area and the other half in Mount Rainier National Park. Hike in a clockwise direction and keep right at

Burnt browns and reds of autumn on the shores of Upper Tipsoo Lake.

any trail junctions. At Tipsoo Lake one can hike a trail from the lake back up to Chinook Pass or the road for .5 miles to your car.

My mom describes below our short evening walk in September of 1998.

Starting at 5:30 p.m. at Chinook Pass we hiked on a good trail of gentle grades, passing tiny streams, miniature waterfalls and boulder gardens. Flowers were past their prime but there were a few Lewis monkey flowers, an occasional magenta paintbrush, partridge foot and groundsel. Small Engelmann spruce and mountain hemlock grew along the trail. Presently a small tarn appeared holding dark reflections and rimmed with a strip of brown earth. Twisted stumps and bleached snags added to the

Hiker ambles through a meadow of dishmops at the close of the day.

timberline character of the trail. As we rounded the southeast side of the peak, Mt. Adams and the Goat Rocks came into view.

Hiking westward, we descended on many waterbars and past "Old Men of the Mountain" (anemone flowers that have gone to seed) catching the golden light of evening. One valiant clump of violet-blue harebells waved slightly in the gentle breeze. All along here we were on a high ridge overlooking haze-filled valleys and timbered hills.

We by now had almost circled Naches Peak, coming out on its northwest side; the trail then descended through sub-alpine firs to an open area where the path widened. A panorama unfolded of Mt. Rainier and Tipsoo Lake. We passed a smaller lake not far above the highway, full of warm greens and ochre-yellows, mirroring the mellow colors of the season.

It was about 7 p.m. as we finished and I let Alan complete the final part of the loop by walking the road uphill to the car. To the west the glacier-clad volcano began to slip into the shadows as lavender painted the sky.

22 SUMMERLAND

Round Trip: 8.4 miles

Elevation Gain: 2000 feet

A trip into Summerland will reward one with lush meadows of wildflowers, high windswept slopes at Panhandle Gap and possibly mountain goats. If one is able to get a backcountry permit and camp overnight, the morning and evening play of light in the meadows and on the mountain is well worth the stay.

Approach as for Hike 20 and continue .4 mile farther on Hwy. 410 to the White River junction. Go right on the White River/Sunrise Road and drive 4 miles beyond the junction and through the White River entrance to the park, to Frying Pan Creek (23 miles from Greenwater). Park in a lot on the right. The trail to Summerland starts on the left (south side of road) and parallels the west side of Frying Pan Creek. Go straight at .1 mile and follow the trail through an old hemlock forest with side streams cleaving the mossy ground. Cross Frying Pan Creek in a little over 3 miles, where avalanche paths have been scoured by winter snows.

Louseworts and lupine on a misty morning in Summerland.

The trail switchbacks the last bit up to Summerland gaining 700 feet. Incredible meadows are laced by streams flanked by bright green moss and monkey flowers. I have been into Summerland twice: for three days during August of 1998 and for several days with my parents in 1966. Even today this trip from my youth stands out in my memory as a unique visit to the alpine world.

We backpacked in for four days and my dad had the brilliant idea it would be easier if I pushed part of our load on a makeshift wheelbarrow that was once used for carrying firewood. He reasoned that this "technique" would save our shoulders from those bone-crushing loads. What it did was completely trash my forearms, since it was I who pushed the load most of the way. Once in Summerland we stayed in the stone shelter along with hoards of mice and occasional Wonderland Trail overnighters. One family was carrying with them all of the food for the 90 mile trek without any resupplies along the way. They were tired, irritable and overly concerned that everyone's cooking utensils would get mixed up at suppertime.

During the day, we hiked up to Panhandle Gap and explored the nooks and crannies of the adjacent slopes and woods. Dad had brought his Pentax SLR with a screw-mount 50mm lens and got great photos of a mother ptarmigan shepherding her chicks among the rocks. The film he used back then was the venerable Kodachrome II with an asa of 25. Mom took time at breaks to sketch and paint watercolors of the mountain splendor. We also saw mountain goats, swatted mosquitoes and ate plenty of rye crisp and kipper snacks for lunch.

All I recall about the hike out is that the load did not seem much lighter to my already fatigued arms.

The author with the "wheelbarrow" and his parents in Summerland, 1966.

TY KEARNEY PHOTO

The past is a blur, where the time has gone
who can say.
The memories of our youth ripen with age.
And although our bodies lack the same
spring or resiliency,
they can still walk the meadows, the high
ridges and gaze
at the peaks.
For new memories added to old, enhance
and crystallize
the beauty of the mountains.

Bands of monkey flowers are backlit by early evening stormy light in Summerland.

A deer browses in a lush meadow.

23 BURROUGHS MOUNTAIN

Round Trip: 11.2 miles
Elevation Gain: 3000 feet

The Burroughs Mountain loop offers incredible vistas of the Emmons and Winthrop Glaciers and Goat Island Mountain to the south. Burroughs Mountain is the remnant of an ancient lava flow that partly filled the canyon of White River. The high open and rocky slopes on top are the home of hardy lichens and small alpine flowers such as shrubby cinquefoil, stonecrop, moss campion and dwarf lupine.

Approach as for Hike 22 and drive another 1 mile more along the White River/Sunrise Road to the junction of White River Campground and Sunrise. Turn left and continue another mile to the end of the road and park on the left in a lot within the campground. Walk to the west end of the road and hike the Glacier Basin Trail for 2.4 miles in 1300 feet. Turn right and head up the Burroughs Mountain Trail, gaining 1800 feet to the top in about 3 miles.

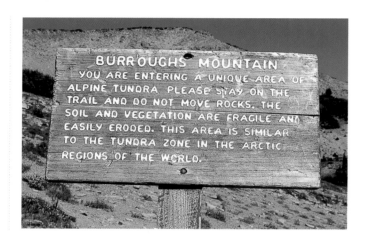

A spectacular view of Frying Pan Glacier, Little Tahoma and the serpentine Emmons Glacier from Burroughs Mountain.

Author running to the rocky tip of Burroughs Mountain.

From the summit, descend eastward for .6 mile and go right at the junction toward Sunrise Camp. In 1.4 miles keep right at Sunrise Camp and in another .9 mile go right again and hike 2.6 miles down to White River Campground. This forms a clockwise loop and a long hike: it can be especially hot and dry on a summer day so plenty of fluids are essential.

I did the hike in July of 1998 as a trail run. It was a perfect day so I carried only the minimum of water, snacks, windshirt and camera. I started early when it was cool and stopped at the first junction for a water break and a stretch. My "run" is more of a plod and the whole trip took 3 hours and 15 minutes (including 25 minutes worth of stops for photos). On top I propped my camera on a boulder, set the self timer and shot photos of myself running up through the final boulders.

It began to get warm on the descent and my sweaty feet began to develop hot spots. I stopped quickly and put several strips of athletic tape on the bottom of my feet, which solved the problem. Beware of letting chafed feet go untended. Blisters can develop quickly and make for an agonizing walk.

My biggest complaint with running a trail is there isn't much time for shooting photos and really enjoying the surroundings in a leisurely manner. But it is a different way to experience the mountains and after a long break at the car, I did a short easy hike later that afternoon.

A hardy alpine meadow.

24 YAKIMA PARK

Round Trip: 2.4 miles

Elevation Gain: 200 feet

The short hike down to Yakima Park is easy and provides excellent views of the Emmons Glacier and White River. It is an ideal place at dawn to shoot the low-angle, warm light on the mountain.

Approach as for Hike 22 and from the White River Campground junction continue up the Sunrise Road for another 11 miles (35 miles from Greenwater) to Sunrise. From the southwest end of the parking lot take the trail to Emmons Vista. Hike downhill .1 mile and go left on a nearly level trail to Yakima Park.

At Emmons Vista there is a geological display and the best view of the largest mass of ice in the lower 48 states: the combined ice streams of the Emmons and Winthrop Glaciers. The Emmons is 5 miles in length (Rainier's largest glacier), the Winthrop emanates just

below the summit of the mountain and descends to 4700 feet. The Emmons Glacier advanced (accumulation of snow exceeded ablation [melting] and the glacier grew) during 1953 and the late 1960s. But overall the glacier's snout has receded over a mile since 1900. When observing a glacier look for the "firn" limit, that demarcation between the "zone of accumulation" and "zone of ablation". Generally it is an uneven line with cleaner firn (old snow changing to denser sphericals of granular ice) snow above and dirty glacier ice below.

If one makes an early morning hike of it, Yakima Park offers expansive views with grassy meadows that glow golden early in the day. Here a warming filter or a warm polarizer is a good choice for shooting the grass in the foreground and the mountain behind. I

Stormy dawn light on Mount Rainier from Yakima Park.

Subalpine firs and alpenglow in the Emmons Glacier from Yakima Park.

have been to Yakima Park several times and a solid tripod is handy for steadying the camera and lens in the morning breeze. Row upon row of spearlike sub-alpine firs form a striking contrast to the soft curves of the mountains' shape and flowing glaciers.

On one visit to the park I shot some deliberately blurred images of the scene just to see how they would look: an impressionistic approach if you will. I kept notes on the various techniques I employed but to date I still prefer the mountain and trees rendered sharp.

Remnant snags of a forest fire on the path to Yakima Park.

25 DEGE PEAK

Round Trip: 3.4 miles

Elevation Gain: 900 feet

Round Trip: Bike 2.5 miles

Dege and Antler Peaks lie along Sourdough Ridge just northeast and above Sunrise. From the 7006-foot Dege Peak one gets great views of the Frying Pan, Emmons and Winthrop glaciers to the west, Grand Park to the northwest and on a clear day, Mt. Baker and Glacier Peak to the north.

Approach as for Hike 24 and ditch a bike at Sunrise for the return ride down to Sunrise Point. Drive 2.5 miles back down the road to Sunrise Point to begin the hike or (if doing a Round Trip: hike of 6.8 miles from Sunrise Point, start and end the hike there). From Sunrise Point the trail starts at the northwest end of the parking lot and follows a narrow ridge for half a mile. The path then traverses the south side of Dege Peak until at 1 mile, you take a right at the junction and hike a short distance to the top.

Descend from Dege Peak and continue west on the Sourdough Ridge Trail for another 1.3 miles then go left and down toward Sunrise. In .4 mile more go left again and walk .3 mile to Sunrise and get on your bike. Otherwise retrace your route back to Sunrise Point for the longer and bikeless version of the hike.

This is a short and pleasant trip that I did by myself in the summer of 1998. As I was tired from previous exercise I found it just the right activity for my mood. Especially in the early morning it is a fantastic place to shoot the early light on the mountain. As a photographer I have always tried to tune into the seasons and "the pulse of nature" as the famous landscape photographer David Muench put it. Being constantly aware of nature's disposition is essential in capturing good landscape photographs. The moods of stormy weather, sudden snowfalls, exceptional flower displays or autumn colors more brilliant than in other years, lend a rich medium to create your images from.

It is also fun to develop a favorite spot in the outdoors and return to it again and again-shooting its different moods and changes. If you take a tripod and record the same scene with the same lens and composition, you can create a visual story of that place. In so doing you learn what happens to your subject when light strikes it at different times of the day and how the plants change with the seasons. Used in a slide program, such a record of one place is impressive.

Right: Yakima Park, Emmons and Winthrop glaciers from Dege Peak.
Below: Hikers taking a break on Dege Peak.

26 MT. FREMONT LOOKOUT

Round Trip: 6 miles

Elevation Gain: 1000 feet

Hiker leaving Sunrise early for the journey to Mt. Fremont.

Mt. Fremont Lookout offers exceptional vistas of the east and north side of Mt. Rainier including Curtis Ridge, the Carbon Glacier, Willis Wall and Liberty Ridge. The broad sweep of Grand Park lies just to the north. Mountain Goats frequent the rocky slopes in this area as well.

Approach as for Hikes 24 and 25. From the northwest end of the Sunrise parking lot, take the trail up toward Antler Peak and Mt. Fremont. Keep left at .3 mile, .5 mile and .9 miles. Follow the Sourdough Ridge Trail west to the junction of Burroughs Mtn., Berkeley Park and Mt. Fremont. Go right toward Mt. Fremont and hike another 1.3 miles up over a rocky path to the fire lookout.

I hiked with a friend in September of 1998 on a clear, cool day where the streamers of approaching storm clouds had begun to lace the sky. We encountered a herd of 22 mountain goats on the northwestern slope below the lookout. Their white fur was beginning to grow thick again as protection from winter's approaching icy breath. They were munching on small grasses and lichens and were not disturbed by the presence of a half dozen hikers who respectfully kept their distance from the animals. There were several families of goats that included frisky kids bounding from boulder to boulder on the uneven terrain.

I shot photos of the goats using a 70 - 300mm f 4 - f 5.6 Nikkor zoom on a four pound tripod and Fujichrome Sensia 100 speed film. Some of the images were shot with the lens at 200mm to show a whole string of goats and others at 300mm to get in closer. When photographing animals, it is important to wait until they look right at you so you can focus on the eyes before shooting. Locking the mirror up on the camera body and using a cable release to dampen vibration insured getting sharp photos of the nimble creatures.

When in the mountains we do not often think of nature in motion. When we finally pause and look around, we notice it. The crumbling ice wall of a glacial serac, wind-whipped dust racing across a slope or the white blur of a running goat all remind us that nature is indeed not static.

Winter's coming.
Autumn snows blanket the mountains preparing
them with winter's mantle of white.
I want summer memories to cover me with warmth
and ward off the cold fingers of winter.

Opposite page and below: Mountain goats on the slopes of Mt. Fremont.

27 MYSTIC LAKE

Round Trip: 27 miles*
Elevation Gain: 4700 feet

*(14.6 miles when Carbon River Road is open and hike begins at Ipsut Creek Campground)

From Mystic Lake one gets a breathtaking look at Mt. Rainier's great north face, comprised of the Willis Wall and its huge ice cliff, Liberty Ridge and Liberty Wall. Mystic Lake and adjacent tarns are one of the more enchanting places found on the mountain. Camping in the area is limited and by permit only.

Approach this hike from Enumclaw and drive south on Hwy. 165 to Carbonado. Three miles past Carbonado go left on the Carbon River Road to Fairfax. From Fairfax it is 5.8 miles more to the Carbon River Entrance to the park. Until the Carbon River Road is opened to Ipsut Creek Campground, one must start hiking at the entrance. From the entrance hike 6 miles to the Ipsut Creek Campground and then follow the Wonderland Trail for 7.5 miles to Mystic Lake. Keep on the main trail which parallels the Carbon river on the west for 2.9 miles. Cross the bridge over to the east bank and hike 4.6 miles more to Mystic Lake.

I backpacked into Mystic Lake in 1976 with the hopes of climbing Liberty Ridge. It was July and fairly warm; the snow was not freezing during the night. My climbing partner had just returned from climbing in Yosemite Valley and was exhausted from all night driving. We got a late start for our climb and turned back due to unsafe conditions. We lolled around the lake in the afternoon and then hiked out. As I was carrying climbing and camping gear, I did not have a tripod with me and missed getting sharp landscape photos.

For good scenic images it is wise to include a bit of foreground in the composition to give depth to the scene. In order to have good sharpness from foreground to background it is essential to use a small opening (aperture) on your lens. A small aperture (f 16 or f 22) does not let much light reach the film so one must use slower shutter speeds-and hence a tripod-for sharp results. Sometimes one can improvise in a pinch by bracing the camera against a tree trunk, or propping it on top of a boulder and then squeezing the shutter very slowly, or using the camera's self timer to trigger the shutter.

Remember, although high speed films (asa 200 or 400) will allow you to shoot in daylight with small apertures, the color and sharpness of those films is inferior to slower films like Fujichrome Velvia.

Seventeen years after my first trip to Mystic Lake and Liberty Ridge I returned in the winter with two friends to try the climb again. After two days of approaching on skis, we climbed to 13,000 feet on the ridge on our third day. Out of time and daylight we descended the ridge in the dark and skied out the fourth day. The north side of the mountain was like another world in winter; lifeless, desolate and incredibly beautiful. We found only a frozen expanse of ice and snow where Mystic Lake was; quite different from the friendly pond backpackers experience in the summer.

Ptarmigan on the shores of Mystic Lake.

Have you hiked in the high places?
Where the wind blows away your cares
and the sun penetrates every fiber.
Where rock, snow and ice are honed
to perfection in the alpine realm.
Where time seems frozen
and the rest of the world is distant.

Opposite page: Climbers admire Willis Wall and Liberty from Mystic Lake.
Below: Liberty Ridge rises above heather slopes in autumn.

28 GOLDEN LAKES

Round Trip: 20 miles

Elevation Gain: 3500 feet

The lakes consist of over a dozen beautiful ponds and tarns nestled among hemlocks and cedars. Enroute to the lakes one gets rare views of the northwest side of the mountain including the North Mowich Glacier, Edmunds Glacier, Sunset Ridge and South Mowich Glacier.

Approach as for Hike 27. Three miles south of Carbonado keep right on the Mowich Lake Road. Follow the Mowich Lake Road 12 miles to the Paul Peak Picnic Area. Take the Paul Peak Trail and drop 700 feet in 3.4 miles down to the junction of the Wonderland Trail. Go right and hike another mile down 400 feet to the South Mowich River. Climb 2100 feet in 3.5 miles to a ridge with good views of the mountain. From there the path gains another 400 feet over 2.1 miles to the lakes. Backcountry permits are required for camping at the lakes.

I backpacked into Golden Lakes during mid-October of 1998 and trudged through several inches of slushy snow the last 3 miles. I arrived just in time to catch the last glowing colors filtering through storm clouds and illuminating the Mowich Face on Mt. Rainier. Since the lakes were in dark shadow, I used a split density filter to hold back the light from the bright mountain and allow the lesser light from the lakes to reach the film. Without the filter the mountain would be just the right exposure (if that is where you took your light meter reading) and the lakes would be inky black without any detail.

I was lucky to get any view of the peak since more thick clouds were moving in quickly. It snowed during the night and—typical for Northwest weather—it turned to rain by morning. After a quick breakfast and a steaming hot drink, I packed, then spent an hour shooting close-ups of leaves and grass on the shores of one of the larger lakes. On the way out I crossed fresh cougar tracks in the snow. It looked as though the big cat had crossed the trail just that morning leaving four inch wide prints in the snow. Not being a large person anyway, I was wondering how I might have appeared big and threatening had I encountered the cougar.

Opposite page: A brief clearing during an October storm illuminates Mount Rainier from Golden Lakes.

29 TOLMIE PEAK

Round Trip: 7 miles

Elevation Gain: 1400 feet

The hike up to Tolmie Peak and the old fire lookout is not long and offers incredible views of Eunice Lake and the northwest side of Mt. Rainier. From the peak one can see the glistening ice walls and snowslopes of the Willis Wall, Liberty Ridge, Ptarmigan Ridge and Mowich Face.

Approach as for Hike 28 and drive 5 miles more to Mowich Lake and park at the south end. From here follow the trail 1.7 miles around the west side of the lake and gain 700 feet to Ipsut Pass. At Ipsut Pass go left and hike another 1.8 miles past Eunice Lake (a dish of bedrock carved out by ice 15,000 to 20,000 years ago) and 700 feet more up to Tolmie Peak.

Eight years ago I hiked to the peak in late afternoon, trying to get unusual light on the mountain. The autumn foliage was bright red along the path and the September day cool and clear. At the top a stiff breeze was blowing so I donned all my extra clothes and dug out a thermos of hot cocoa. I got my camera and tripod all set up (for that trip a Pentax 6x7cm) and waited for the evening light. A bright, nearly full moon began to rise over the mountain as the snowslopes glowed rosy-orange.

I used a polarizing filter to darken the sky and richen the colors of the snow. Since I was using a 300mm on the 6x7cm (equal to a 150mm on a 35mm SLR) for some of the images, the sharpest pictures were those where the exposures were several seconds long or longer: this reduced the vibration from the camera's shutter. I always like to wait until the very last colors have faded away before packing up the equipment. You never know what surprises the light has in store until the end. Sometimes evening colors will be reflected off clouds in the sky or the sun will pop between cloud layers at just the last moment providing striking and unusual photos.

I waited until I was shivering with cold, put on my headlamp and hiked the well-maintained trail back to Mowich Lake and the car.

Moon rising above the Mowich face of Mount Rainier.

Opposite page: Glacier-carved Eunice Lake below Tolmie Peak.

30 SPRAY PARK

Round Trip: 6 miles

Elevation Gain: 2500 feet

A hike into Spray Park just after the snow melts can provide one the Mt. Rainier's best displays of avalanche lilies. In addition, the impressive Willis Wall rises in a 3,600-foot unbroken sweep to just below the mountain's false summit of Liberty Cap.

Approach as for Hike 29 and park at the south end of Mowich Lake. Hike south a short distance to the junction of the Wonderland Trail and go left toward Spray Park. The trail drops 300 feet past several incredible side streams, one of which is a very photogenic collection of lush mossy rocks and rivulets of clear water. The trail then climbs back up past Spray Falls and into Spray Park.

If the flower meadows are not quite in full bloom and the weather good, one of my favorite activities in the mountains is to find a comfortable boulder to lean against and get out my small binoculars. In Spray Park, on several occasions, I have taken a break and studied the Willis Wall with its layers of lava flows, steep snowslopes and the daunting 300-foot ice cliff at the top.

Resembling a piedmont glacier, the ice sheet continually pushes its mass of ice outward until gravity finally takes hold and huge chunks break off. Glacier flow is a result of basal sliding (ice in contact with bedrock and moving) and is much greater in summer due to stored water in the fall, winter and spring. When an icefall (a greatly accelerated flow of ice down an abnormally steep slope) does occur the resulting spectacle and thundering noise is another example of nature in a constant state of change.

Photographing an ice avalanche (not to be confused with a snow slab avalanche) is a tricky thing to capture. Get a light meter reading beforehand, expose 1 - 1.5 f stops over the bright snow (if the meter says f 11 shoot at f 8 or between f 5.6 and f 8) and use a high shutter speed (1,000 of a second) to freeze the action.

I never have photographed a good avalanche off the Willis Wall on several trips to Spray Park but have been content to relax and admire nature's beauty.

Verdant moss cloaks boulders on a trailside stream en route to Spray Park.

Alpine Field Notes

Sunlight flushes open alpine fields,
steep, sprawling meadows congested with wildflowers.
Here, magenta paintbrush,
Pearly everlasting and goldenrod absorb the warm
Autumnal sun.
Above, the heather, those compact survivors
of winter's avalanches, cling eternally to rocky earth.

Kathy Swindler   1998

FURTHER READING

A Year In Paradise, Floyd Schmoe. Tuttle, Tokyo, 1968.

Cascade Alpine Guide: Columbia River to Stevens Pass (second edition), Fred Beckey.
The Mountaineers, Seattle, 1986.

Cascade - Olympic Natural History, Daniel Matthews. Raven Editions, Portland, 1988.

Glaciers, Robert P. Sharp. University of Oregon Press, Eugene, 1960.

Mountain Light, Galen Rowell. Sierra Club Books, San Francisco, 1986.

The Canoe and the Saddle, Theodore Winthrop (edited by John Williams). Franklin-
Ward, Portland, 1913.